THE POINTLESS BOOK 3

CREATED BY ALFIE DEYES, LOVED BY YOU

Bluestreak
BOOKS

PUBLISHED IN NORTH AMERICA BY BLUE STREAK BOOKS
AN IMPRINT OF WELDON OWEN
WELDON OWEN IS A DIVISION OF BONNIER PUBLISHING USA
1045 SANSOME STREET, SUITE 100, SAN FRANCISCO, CA 94111
WWW.WELDONOWEN.COM

LIBRARY OF CONGRESS CATALOGING IN PUBLICATION DATA IS AVAILABLE.

ISBN: 978-1-68188-361-8

FIRST PRINTED IN GREAT BRITAIN BY BLINK PUBLISHING
THE EDITION FIRST PRINTED IN 2017
1 3 5 7 9 10 8 6 4 2

PRINTED IN CANADA

DESIGNED BY EMILY ROUGH,
ALL IMAGES COPYRIGHT SHUTTERSTOCK

THE POINTLESS BOOK 3
APP

SCAN THE PAGE
WHEN YOU SEE THE
PHONE ICON!

I'M SURE YOU ALL KNOW HOW IT WORKS BY NOW. YOU CAN
ACCESS THE FREE APP FROM ITUNES OR GOOGLE PLAY;
THEN POINT YOUR DEVICE AT THE PAGES THAT DISPLAY
THE SPECIAL ICON – THE VIDEOS WILL THEN BE REVEALED
ON-SCREEN! THE APP ALSO INCLUDES MORE ACTIVITIES
COMPLETED BY ALFIE!

THE POINTLESS BOOK APP REQUIRES AN INTERNET
CONNECTION TO BE DOWNLOADED, AND CAN BE USED ON
MOST IPHONE, IPAD OR ANDROID DEVICES. FOR DIRECT LINKS
TO DOWNLOAD THE APP AND FURTHER INFORMATION,
VISIT WWW.BLINKPUBLISHING.CO.UK.

LIFE GOALS

MONEY

- ○
- ○
- ○

CAREER

PERSONAL LIFE

BUCKET LIST

SOCIAL LIFE

FAMILY

THE SIX DEGREES OF SEPARATION GAME

THINK OF TWO NAMES. NOW CONNECT THEM TOGETHER USING ONLY SIX OTHER NAMES. YOU CAN PLAY IT WITH ACTORS, WHERE EACH ACTOR HAS TO BE CONNECTED BY A FILM, OR MUSICIANS, WRITERS, OR SPORTSPEOPLE!

DOODLE PAGE

TRY SOME OTHER DRAWINGS HERE!

COPY DRAWINGS WITH A PEN IN YOUR MOUTH

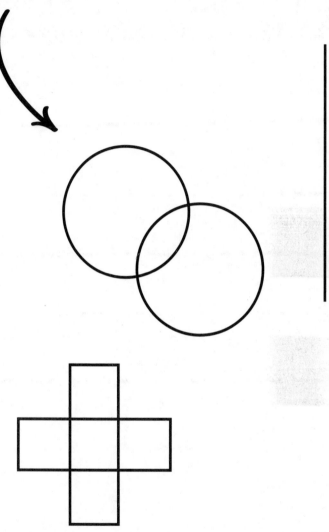

SCAN THE PAGE TO SEE
ALFIE'S ATTEMPT

HANGMAN

GRAB A FRIEND, THINK OF SOME WORDS AND PLAY HANGMAN.

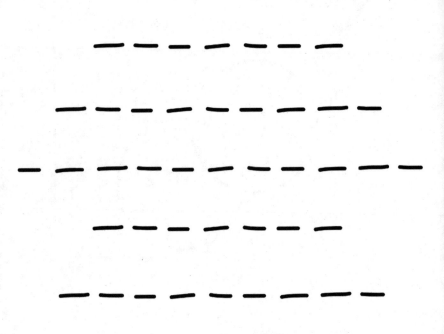

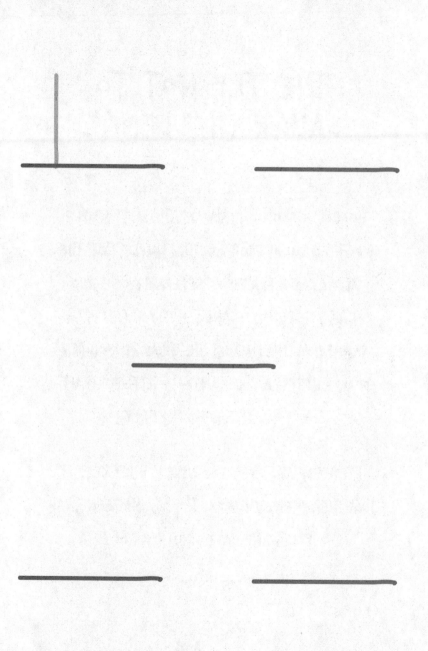

THE TRY NOT TO LAUGH CHALLENGE

THE BEST GAMES ARE ALWAYS THE MOST SIMPLE. AND THIS GAME IS PROBABLY THE SIMPLEST OF THEM ALL! GRAB A FRIEND — PREFERABLY ONE WHO FINDS YOU FUNNY — AND SEE IF YOU CAN DRAW SOMETHING THAT MAKES THEM LAUGH. YOU CAN DRAW WHATEVER YOU WANT — A SELF-PORTRAIT, A STUPID PICTURE — ANYTHING!

IF THEY LAUGH THEN YOU WIN; IF THEY KEEP IT TOGETHER THEN, UNLUCKY, TRY AGAIN! THEN SWAP ROLES AND HAVE ANOTHER GO!

HERE'S SOME PAPER FOR THE TRY NOT TO LAUGH CHALLENGE

HOW TO DECLUTTER

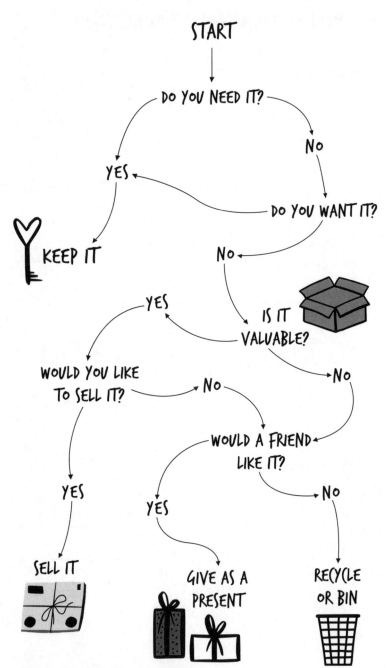

START

DO YOU NEED IT?

NO

YES

DO YOU WANT IT?

KEEP IT

NO

IS IT VALUABLE?

YES

NO

WOULD YOU LIKE TO SELL IT?

NO

WOULD A FRIEND LIKE IT?

YES

YES

NO

SELL IT

GIVE AS A PRESENT

RECYCLE OR BIN

USE THIS PAGE FOR WHEN YOU NEXT HAVE DEJA VU.
WRITE DOWN WHAT HAPPENED!

DAILY GOALS

CAREER

MONEY

SOCIAL LIFE

BUCKET LIST

o

o

o

PERSONAL LIFE

FAMILY

5-YEAR GOALS

MONEY

CAREER

o

o

o

SOCIAL LIFE

BUCKET LIST

PERSONAL LIFE

FAMILY

CREATE

ART BY BETH MCFADZEAN

DARES FOR FRIENDS

GRAB A FEW FRIENDS FOR SOME TRUTH OR DARE.

1. WRITE A DARE FOR EACH OF THE 3 DARE BOXES AND A QUESTION TO ASK FOR THE 3 TRUTH BOXES.

2. CUT OUT THE 9 BOXES AND PLACE THEM FACE DOWN ON A TABLE. MIX THEM AROUND!

3. TAKE TURNS PICKING A CARD. IF IT LANDS ON 'DODGED A BULLET', THEN IT'S THE NEXT PERSON'S TURN TO PICK A CARD.

TRUTH	DARE	DODGED A BULLET

DING BATS

B B B B
A A A A
R R R R
G G G G _____

THE SAND _____

AM**U**OUS _____

SGEG _____

LAW ON _____

SCAN THE PAGE AND WATCH ALFIE'S GUESSES

JUMBLED PARAGRAPH

FI OYU OCME WDON OT BINGHRTO, EB RUSE OT GTE ELFSOURY NA ECI MARCE. A DROW FO GNIRAWN, TOGHUH. ALWAYS PEEK NOE YEE NO ROYU 99 RO A LUGLESA LIWL KNIC TI. TEH SEMA APPLESI OT SHIF DNA PICSH, DYNAC SSLOLF NAD CROK.

IF YOU COME DOWN...

DOT TO DOT

POINTLESS ANAGRAMS!

SEE IF YOU CAN WORK OUT THE REAL PHRASES FROM THE ANAGRAMS BELOW:

DOGGY MOOING RUNS!

_____

AMPLIFY FROCKS OBOE

_____

A HAMMERHEAD WOOFS TOOK YUPPY

_____

BOOKSTORES PILE THEN

_____

DESIGN YOUR OWN COMPANY LOGO

ART BY CHELSIE CROUCHER

BIRTHDAY LIST

THINGS I WOULD LIKE
FOR MY BIRTHDAY:

THINGS I NEED TO REMEMBER TO
BUY OTHER PEOPLE:

PERSONAL Q&A

IN THE SPACE BELOW WRITE A QUESTION ABOUT YOURSELF. IT CAN BE ANYTHING – WHAT'S YOUR FAVORITE THING ABOUT ME? DO YOU LIKE MY HAIR? – AND ASK YOUR FRIENDS FOR AN ANSWER.

QUESTION	ANSWER

QUESTION	ANSWER

QUESTION	ANSWER

QUESTION	ANSWER

QUESTION	ANSWER

OPTICAL ILLUSION

STARE AT THE DOT IN THE MIDDLE OF THE IMAGE FOR 30 SECONDS THEN STARE
AT THE CEILING OR A BLANK PIECE OF PAPER AND START BLINKING.
WHAT DO YOU SEE?

WRITE A HAIKU

A HAIKU IS A 3-LINE TRADITIONAL JAPANESE POEM. THE
FIRST AND THIRD LINES ARE 5 SYLLABLES LONG,
AND THE SECOND LINE 7 SYLLABLES.

EXAMPLE:

BRIGHTON IS MY HOME

I LOVE TO WALK BY THE SEA

AND HANG OUT WITH FRIENDS

 NOW GIVE IT A GO!

THE MOCKTAIL COLLECTION...

 ### OLD PASSIONED

FILL A GLASS WITH ICE, ADD SODA WATER AND A SPLASH OF ORANGE JUICE.

 ### LAST TANGO

FILL THE GLASS WITH TWO PARTS ORANGEADE AND ONE PART SODA. POP AN ORANGE SLICE ON THE SIDE OF THE GLASS TOO!

 ### NOJITO

FILL A GLASS WITH ICE, ADD SODA WATER, A SQUEEZE OF LIME AND SOME MINT.

 ### ESPRESSO-TINI

BREW SOME COFFEE AND LEAVE TO COOL. ADD ICE TO A GLASS, ONE PART COCONUT MILK AND A DROP OF VANILLA ESSENCE. TOP UP WITH THE COFFEE.

 ### BRIGHTON ICED T

BREW SOME RASPBERRY TEA AND COOL DOWN. ADD ICE, STIR WITH SODA WATER AND A SQUEEZE OF LIME AND SERVE.

 ### VIRGIN MARY

ADD SOME ICE TO A GLASS. FILL WITH TOMATO JUICE AND A SPLASH OF WORCESTERSHIRE SAUCE.

 ### APPLE SOUR

FILL THE GLASS WITH TWO PARTS SPARKLING APPLE CIDER AND ONE PART SODA WATER. POP IN SOME ICE CUBES TOO!

 ### POINTLESS PUNCH

MIX PINEAPPLE JUICE AND ORANGE JUICE. POUR INTO A GLASS FILLED WITH ICE AND TOP UP WITH SODA WATER.

DESIGN YOUR OWN TATTOO!

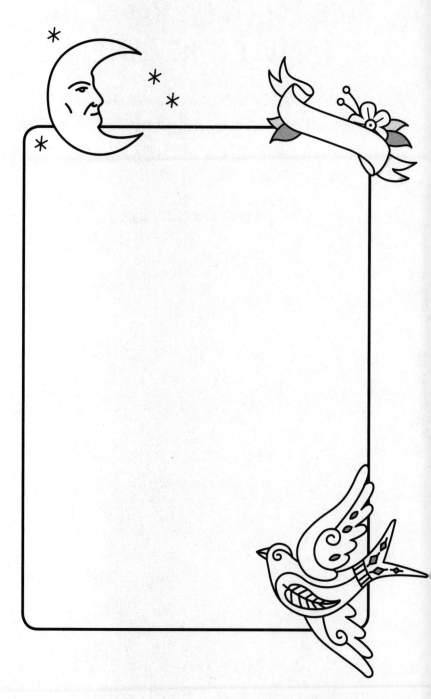

THE POINTLESS BOOK TIME CAPSULE... REVISITED!

DO YOU REMEMBER THE TIME CAPSULE PAGES FROM
THE POINTLESS BOOK? REMEMBER I ASKED YOU TO WRITE SOMETHING
ON THE PAGES AND STICK THEM TOGETHER? WELL... WHY NOT GO
AND OPEN THEM UP AND CHECK OUT WHAT YOU WROTE?

JOT DOWN YOUR SECRET HERE

HYGGE PAGE

HYGGE IS A NEW TREND FROM DENMARK THAT FOCUSES ON GETTING THE BEST OUT OF LIFE'S EVERYDAY MOMENTS OR SIMPLE PLEASURES, SUCH AS FAMILY, FRIENDS OR SPENDING TIME ON YOUR OWN AND READING A GOOD BOOK.

WRITE DOWN ALL OF YOUR FAVORITE HYGGE MOMENTS BELOW AND REFLECT BACK ON THIS PAGE WHENEVER YOU NEED SOME 'YOU' TIME…

LEARN TO SAY HELLO IN 9 DIFFERENT LANGUAGES

YOU NEVER KNOW WHEN IT MIGHT COME IN HANDY...

SALAAM
(FARSI)

NAMASTE
(HINDI)

ZDR-AVS-TVUY-TE
(RUSSIAN)

KONNICHIWA
(JAPANESE)

JAMBO
(SWAHILI)

NI HAU
(MANDARIN)

AHN-NYONG-HA-SE-YO
(SOUTH KOREAN)

SZIA
(HUNGARIAN)

YASOU
(GREEK)

THE MOCKTAIL COLLECTION...
ICED TEA!

MAKE YOUR OWN ICED TEA USING THE RECIPE BELOW:

INGREDIENTS

2 ½ CUPS WATER

3 TEABAGS

1 TABLESPOON SUGAR

2 TABLESPOONS CONDENSED MILK

ICE

METHOD

BOIL THE WATER AND ADD TO A SAUCEPAN

ADD THE TEABAGS AND LEAVE TO BREW FOR 10 MINS

ADD THE SUGAR AND STIR UNTIL IT'S DISSOLVED

LET THE TEA COOL

FILL TWO TALL GLASSES WITH ICE CUBES

FILL ALL THE WAY UP WITH THE TEA

ADD A TABLESPOON OF CONDENSED MILK TO EACH GLASS AND STIR

DRINK!

MAKE ANOTHER ONE!

SCAN THE PAGE TO SEE
ALFIE'S ATTEMPT

FAVORITE PEOPLE TO FOLLOW ON...

WRITE DOWN YOUR FAVORITE PEOPLE THAT YOU FOLLOW ON:

YOUTUBE

1.

2.

3.

TWITTER

1.

2.

3.

INSTAGRAM

1.

2.

3.

IF I WAS A WORLD LEADER I WOULD...

1.

2.

3.

4.

5.

6.

7.

8.

9.

10.

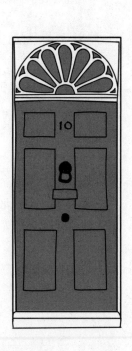

A TRICKY QUIZ

1. HOW MANY MONTHS HAVE 28 DAYS?

_____

2. WHY CAN'T A MAN MARRY HIS WIDOW'S SINGLE SISTER?

_____

3. ALICE'S MOTHER HAD THREE CHILDREN. THE FIRST CHILD WAS
   CALLED APRIL. THE SECOND CHILD WAS CALLED MAY. WHAT WAS
   THE THIRD CHILD'S NAME?

_____

4. BEFORE MOUNT EVEREST WAS DISCOVERED, WHAT WAS THE
   HIGHEST MOUNTAIN IN THE WORLD?

_____

5. HOW CAN SOMEONE GO 8 DAYS WITHOUT SLEEP?

_____

SEND A POSTCARD TO A FAMILY MEMBER OR FRIEND

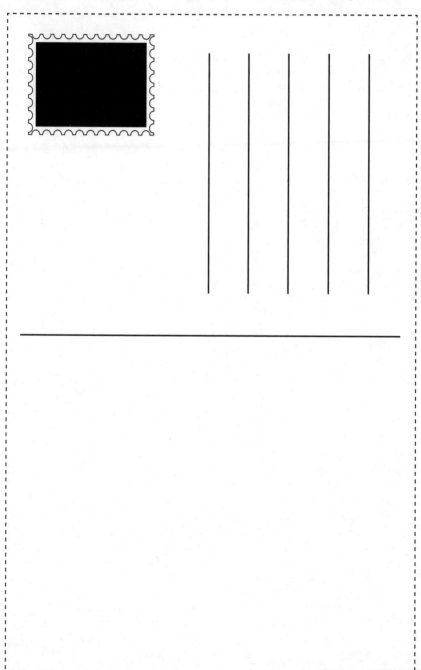

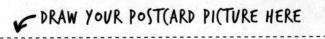 DRAW YOUR POSTCARD PICTURE HERE

LOVE CALCULATOR

HERE IS AN AMUSINGLY COMPLICATED WAY TO WORK OUT WHETHER
YOU AND SOMEONE ELSE ARE GOING TO WORK OUT:

WRITE DOWN HERE:

_____

LOVES

_____

					+
					+
					=

- COUNT UP THE NUMBER OF L, O, V, E, AND S'S IN EACH NAME

- ADD UP THE NUMBERS, PAIR BY PAIR ON THE GRID

- ADD UP TOTALED NUMBERS

- IF YOU END UP WITH NUMBERS ABOVE 10, USE THE LAST DIGIT

- THAT IS YOUR LOVE SCORE

(100% ACCURATE 0% OF THE TIME!)

DRAW YOUR FAMILY TREE

YOU CAN ASK AN ELDERLY RELATIVE TO HELP YOU OUT.

PICTURE PUNS

CAN YOU GUESS THE CAPTIONS FROM THESE PICTURE PUNS?
I'VE HELPED YOU OUT WITH THE FIRST ONE...

1.

ANSWER: GRATEFUL

2.

3.

4.

"YOU CAN DO IT!"

5.

_____

6.

_____

7.

_____

8.

_____

GOOD DEEDS TO DO TODAY

1. OPEN A DOOR FOR SOMEONE ☐

2. PICK UP SOME GARBAGE FROM THE STREET ☐

3. PLEDGE MONEY FOR SOMEONE DOING SOMETHING ☐

4. GIVE SOMETHING TO CHARITY ☐

5. GIVE MONEY TO A STREET PERFORMER ☐

6. LEAVE A LITTLE NOTE FOR A FRIEND TO TELL THEM ☐
   HOW MUCH THEY MEAN TO YOU

7. ☐

8. ☐

9. ☐

MINDFULNESS EXERCISE

MINDFULNESS IS
SO IMPORTANT THESE DAYS.
THE ABILITY TO SWITCH OFF AND BE PART
OF THE PRESENT – WITHOUT THINKING TOO MUCH ABOUT
THE PAST OR THE FUTURE, OR WORRYING ABOUT ANY-
THING – CAN REALLY BE UNDERESTIMATED.

FOR THIS PAGE I'D LIKE YOU TO PUT YOUR PENS OR
PENCILS DOWN AND SIT FOR TEN MINUTES IN COMPLETE
SILENCE, FOCUSING ON YOUR BREATHING. TRY AND DO
THIS A FEW TIMES A WEEK.

DESIGN YOUR MOVIE POSTER

10 NEW WORDS

DID YOU KNOW THAT YOUTUBER WAS ADDED TO THE OXFORD ENGLISH DICTIONARY IN DECEMBER 2016? HERE ARE 10 WEIRD AND WONDERFUL REAL WORDS THAT YOU MAY NOT BE AS FAMILIAR WITH. SEE IF YOU CAN MATCH THEM WITH THEIR DEFINITIONS AND CHECK OUT THE ANSWERS AT THE BACK.

1. BLATHERSKITE

2. BOFFOLA

3. DORYPHORE

4. STERNUTATOR

5. GASCONADE

6. FUTZ

7. FUNAMBULIST

8. CACOETHES

9. EUCATASTROPHE

10. MOLLITIOUS

A. SOMEONE WHO TALKS AT GREAT LENGTH WITHOUT MAKING MUCH SENSE

B. A TIGHTROPE WALKER

C. AN URGE TO DO SOMETHING INADVISABLE

D. SOMETHING THAT CAUSES SNEEZING

E. A JOKE THAT GETS A LOUD OR HEARTY LAUGH

F. A PEDANTIC AND ANNOYINGLY PERSISTENT CRITIC OF OTHERS

G. LUXURIOUS

H. EXTRAVAGANT BOASTING

I. TO WASTE TIME

J. A HAPPY ENDING TO A STORY

SCAN THE PAGE TO WATCH ALFIE'S GUESSES

MAKE UP 5 NEW WORDS AND ADD THEIR DEFINITIONS

1.   DEFINITION:

2.   DEFINITION:

3.   DEFINITION:

4.   DEFINITION

5.   DEFINITION

SIT IN A QUIET ROOM OR OUTSIDE
AND COMPLETELY FOCUS ON A
NATURAL OBJECT (E.G. A FLOWER,
A LEAF, A STONE, A CLOUD). JUST
BY STUDYING IT QUIETLY YOU MIGHT
NOTICE SOMETHING YOU'VE NEVER
SEEN BEFORE.

WRITE DOWN SOME GREAT PET NAMES

WRITE DOWN YOUR FAVORITE FILMS

DRAMA:

COMEDY:

HORROR:

ACTION:

ROMANCE:

SCIENCE-FICTION:

FANTASY:

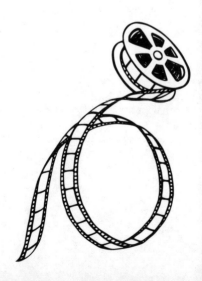

ALPHABET PHONE CALL CHALLENGE

THE IDEA IS TO CALL A FRIEND AND START THE FIRST SENTENCE WITH THE LETTER 'A'.

WHEN THEY REPLY, YOU MUST ANSWER WITH A SENTENCE BEGINNING WITH B AND SO ON. SEE IF YOU CAN (A) GET THROUGH THE ALPHABET AND ALSO (B) COMPLETE IT WITHOUT YOUR FRIEND SUSPECTING THAT YOU'RE UP TO SOMETHING!

MAZE CHALLENGE

START

FINISH

READ ALL ABOUT IT

CUT OUT INDIVIDUAL WORDS AND A PICTURE FROM A NEWSPAPER AND PIECE
TOGETHER YOUR OWN FRONT-PAGE STORY.

DESIGN YOUR OWN WANTED POSTER!

WANTED
DEAD OR ALIVE

SCAN THE PAGE TO SEE
ALFIE'S POSTER

MAKE UP A CODE LANGUAGE

A =   N =

B =   O =

C =   P =

D =   Q =

E =   R =

F =   S =

G =   T =

H =   U =

I =   V =

J =   W =

K =   X =

L =   Y =

M =   Z =

USE YOUR NEW CODE LANGUAGE TO WRITE A MESSAGE TO A FRIEND

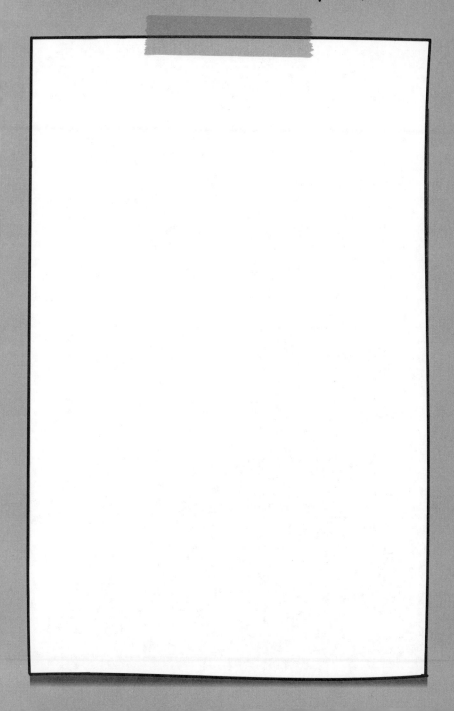

DESIGN YOUR OWN ROLLER COASTER

ASK AN ELDERLY RELATIVE SOMETHING YOU'VE ALWAYS WANTED TO KNOW

HERE ARE SOME IDEAS:

WHAT DID YOU DO WITH YOUR FIRST PAYSLIP?

_____

_____

WHAT'S YOUR EARLIEST MEMORY?

_____

_____

WHO WAS YOUR IDOL WHEN YOU WERE GROWING UP?

_____

_____

WHAT WAS THE FIRST CD OR RECORD YOU BOUGHT?

_____

_____

_____

_____

_____

_____

HOW TO MAKE YOUR OWN BATH BOMB

WANT TO UNWIND AND SAVE YOURSELF SOME MONEY AT THE SAME TIME? HERE'S THE ANSWER...

1 CUP BICARBONATE OF SODA (BAKING SODA)

1/2 CUP CORNFLOUR (CORNSTARCH)

2/3 CUP SEA SALT

1 TBSP OLIVE OIL

1 TSP WATER

FEW DROPS ESSENTIAL OILS (OR LEMON JUICE)

FEW DROPS FOOD COLORING

1 BATH (OBVIOUSLY)

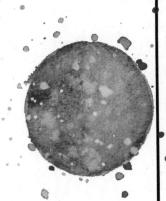

MIX TOGETHER THE DRY INGREDIENTS IN ONE BOWL AND THE WET INGREDIENTS IN ANOTHER BOWL. POUR THE WET INGREDIENTS INTO THE DRY INGREDIENTS AND MIX TOGETHER WELL. PRESS THE MIXTURE INTO A MOLD (OR MOLDS) OF YOUR CHOOSING AND MAKE SURE YOU COMPACT THE MIXTURE TO PREVENT CRACKING. LEAVE THE BATH BOMBS TO DRY FOR AT LEAST 24 HOURS UNTIL THEY'RE DRY TO THE TOUCH.

THEN ADD TO A NICE HOT BATH AND WATCH THE FIZZY FIREWORKS.

FAVORITE YOUTUBER BOOKS

WRITE DOWN YOUR FAVORITE YOUTUBER BOOKS HERE.
I'LL HELP YOU OUT WITH THE FIRST ONE:

- POINTLESS BOOK 3

CREATE A SECRET HANDSHAKE WITH A FRIEND

USE ANY OF THE DRAWINGS BELOW TO HELP YOU OUT

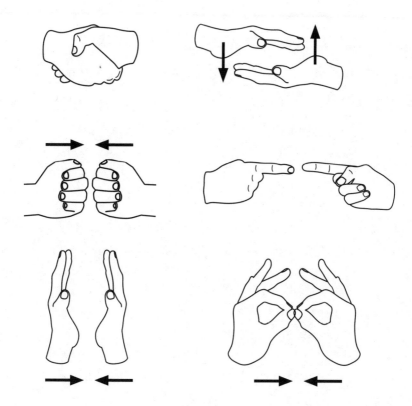

WRITE A LIST OF QUESTIONS YOU'VE ALWAYS WANTED TO ASK YOUR FAVORITE FICTIONAL CHARACTER

(E.G. WHY DIDN'T HERMIONE USE THE TIMETURNER LATER ON IN THE HARRY POTTER BOOKS?!)

GUESS YOUR FUTURE

WRITE DOWN THE ANSWERS TO THE FOLLOWING QUESTIONS AND COME BACK TO THEM IN 10 YEARS' TIME AND SEE IF YOU WERE RIGHT.

IN 10 YEARS I WILL BE LIVING IN:

IN 10 YEARS I WILL BE WITH:

IN 10 YEARS I WILL HAVE TRAVELED TO:

IN 10 YEARS I WILL HAVE WON:

IN 10 YEARS I WILL HAVE MY OWN:

DRAW YOUR FUTURE

DRAW A PICTURE OF YOU OUTSIDE YOUR HOUSE IN 20 YEARS' TIME.

IT'S ORIGAMI TIME

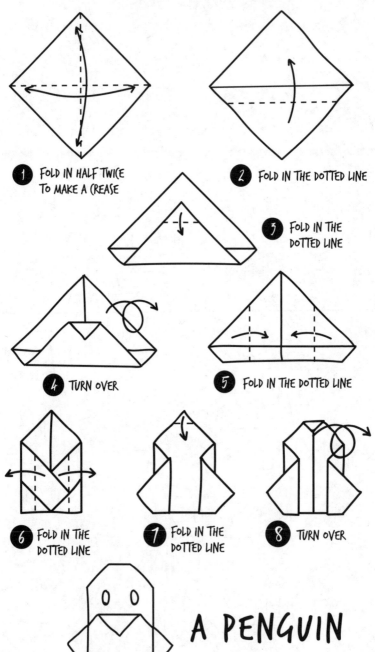

1 FOLD IN HALF TWICE TO MAKE A CREASE

2 FOLD IN THE DOTTED LINE

3 FOLD IN THE DOTTED LINE

4 TURN OVER

5 FOLD IN THE DOTTED LINE

6 FOLD IN THE DOTTED LINE

7 FOLD IN THE DOTTED LINE

8 TURN OVER

A PENGUIN

USE THIS PAGE TO MAKE ORIGAMI!

HERE ARE THE ORIGAMI SQUARES TO (UT OUT

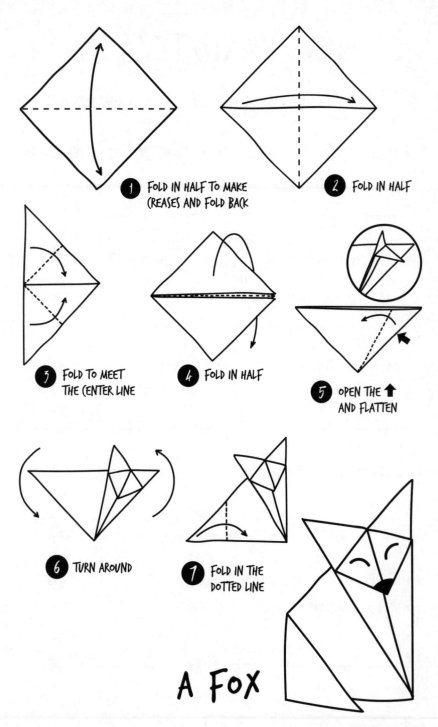

1 FOLD IN HALF TO MAKE CREASES AND FOLD BACK

2 FOLD IN HALF

3 FOLD TO MEET THE CENTER LINE

4 FOLD IN HALF

5 OPEN THE ↑ AND FLATTEN

6 TURN AROUND

7 FOLD IN THE DOTTED LINE

A FOX

New Brainteasers

SEE IF YOU CAN WORK OUT THESE NEW BRAINTEASERS!

WHERE IS THE ONLY PLACE THAT TODAY COMES BEFORE YESTERDAY?

_____

WHAT KIND OF COAT CAN ONLY BE PUT ON WHEN WET?

_____

WHAT LOSES ITS HEAD IN THE MORNING AND GETS IT BACK AT NIGHT?

_____

WHAT IS SO FRAGILE, EVEN SAYING ITS NAME CAN BREAK IT?

_____

WHAT IS BLACK WHEN YOU BUY IT, RED WHEN YOU USE IT AND GREY
WHEN YOU THROW IT AWAY?

_____

POINTLESS CROSSWORD

ACROSS

1. WHICH LANGUAGE DO THEY SPEAK IN ARGENTINA?

2. WHICH IS THE LARGEST US STATE IN TERMS OF POPULATION?

5. WHAT IS THE CAPITAL CITY OF PORTUGAL?

7. THE SMALLEST COUNTRY IN THE WORLD, VATICAN CITY,
IS SURROUNDED BY WHICH COUNTRY?

9. WHAT IS THE LARGEST COUNTRY IN SOUTH AMERICA?

DOWN

1. WHAT IS THE LARGEST ISLAND IN THE MEDITERRANEAN SEA?

3. LAPLAND IS PART OF WHICH EUROPEAN COUNTRY?

4. MOUNT FUJI IS LOCATED IN WHICH ASIAN COUNTRY?

6. WHICH LINE RUNS THROUGH ZERO DEGREES LATITUDE?

8. WHAT IS THE NAME OF THE RIVER THAT RUNS THROUGH PARIS?

PHONE CALL CHALLENGE
⋛ PHRASES ⋚

CALL UP A FRIEND AND INSERT THE FOLLOWING PHRASES INTO THE CONVERSATION WITHOUT AROUSING SUSPICION. ADD SOME OF YOUR OWN BELOW.

1. JUSTICE FOR BARB.

2. DO THE DAB.

3. YOU KNOW NOTHING, JON SNOW.

4. BOOM, MIC DROP.

5.

6.

7.

8.

ACCENTS CHALLENGE

A YOUTUBE CLASSIC – DO YOUR FINEST IMPRESSION OF SOMEONE TALKING IN ONE OF THE ACCENTS BELOW AND ASK YOUR FRIENDS TO GUESS THE ACCENT!

SCOUSE

GEORDIE

NORTHERN IRISH

COCKNEY

YORKSHIRE

NEW YORK

PIRATE

WORD ASSOCIATION

GRAB A FRIEND. THE AIM OF THIS GAME IS TO START WITH A
WORD AND TAKE TURNS SAYING A WORD ASSOCIATED WITH THE
LAST WORD THAT HAS BEEN SAID. IF ONE OF YOU HESITATES OR
CAN'T THINK OF ANYTHING, THEY LOSE:

SHOES

YOUTUBE

CHICKEN

HEADPHONES

DESIGN YOUR OWN OLD-SCHOOL ALBUM COVER

POINTLESS PERSONALITY TEST

CIRCLE A, B, C OR D FOR EACH OF THE OPTIONS BELOW:

ARE YOU:

A DETERMINED
B LOYAL
C SATISFIED
D PLAYFUL

A LOGICAL
B PASSIONATE
C DECENT
D POPULAR

A RESPONSIBLE
B ROMANTIC
C CHARITABLE
D HAPPY

A GOAL-FOCUSED
B SINCERE
C DIPLOMATIC
D IMPULSIVE

A DECISIVE
B DETAIL-ORIENTED
C PATIENT
D AN EXTROVERT

A RESTLESS
B UP AND DOWN
C PASSIVE
D SPONTANEOUS

A CONFIDENT
B ORGANIZED
C PLEASANT
D CHARISMATIC

A TO THE POINT
B CREATIVE
C ADAPTABLE
D LOUD

A STRONG
B DELIBERATE
C GENTLE
D POSITIVE

A ARROGANT
B WORRIED
C PASSIVE-AGGRESSIVE
D UNRELIABLE

A DEMANDING
B A PERFECTIONIST
C ON THE FENCE
D VAIN

A BOSSY
B SELF-INVOLVED
C HESITANT
D FLIRTY

NOW COUNT UP THE NUMBER OF AS, BS, CS AND DS.

MOSTLY AS - YOU'RE THE LEADER OF THE PACK! YOU'RE CONFIDENT, MOTIVATED AND MAKE YOURSELF HEARD. YOU'RE THE ONE PEOPLE TURN TO WHEN A DECISION NEEDS TO BE MADE.	**MOSTLY BS** - YOU'RE A BORN ROMANTIC! YOU'RE THOUGHTFUL, CREATIVE AND PASSIONATE. YOU LIKE YOUR OWN SPACE, THOUGH, AND MEAN WHAT YOU SAY. YOU HAVE A TENDENCY TO BE YOUR OWN WORST ENEMY AND CAN BE HARD ON YOURSELF.
MOSTLY CS - YOU ARE PRETTY CHILLED OUT AND WANT PEOPLE TO HAVE A GOOD TIME! YOU COULD HAPPILY DO WITHOUT FUSS AND STRESS ALTOGETHER. IT DOES MEAN THAT YOU RUN THE RISK OF BEING TAKEN FOR GRANTED.	**MOSTLY DS** - THE LIFE AND SOUL OF THE PARTY! YOU ARE IMPULSIVE, OPTIMISTIC AND CHATTY. YOU ARE QUITE SELF-MOTIVATED AND A LITTLE UNPREDICTABLE.

WEEKLY PLANNER

MONDAY	**DATE**
TUESDAY	**TO DO**
WEDNESDAY	○
THURSDAY	○
FRIDAY	○
SATURDAY	**DO MORE:**
SUNDAY	

EVENTS

SHOPPING LIST

NOTES

REMINDER

WHICH COFFEE ARE YOU?

ESPRESSO
CALM UNDER PRESSURE. WILLING TO STAND UP AND TAKE THE TOUGH DECISIONS WITHOUT BREAKING A SWEAT.

DOUBLE ESPRESSO
INSPIRATIONAL, CONFIDENT CHARACTER WITH BIG DREAMS. GOOD ON YOU. GO BIG OR GO HOME.

TRIPLE ESPRESSO
PARTY STARTER. CAN BE A BIT SCARY, THOUGH. A RELATIONSHIP WITH A LATTE DRINKER COULD BE A DISASTER.

MOCHA
LOVABLE BUT KEEN TO AVOID BEING HUMILIATED IN PUBLIC. JUST ORDER A HOT CHOCOLATE. IT'S NOT THAT EMBARRASSING.

LATTE
SLOW AND STEADY WINS THE RACE. YOU'RE DEPENDABLE BUT NEED TO LET YOUR HAIR DOWN A LITTLE. BUT YOU KNOW THAT. IT'S PENCILED IN FOR NEXT SUNDAY.

CAPPUCCINO
PROUD AND SOMETHING OF A LONE WOLF. QUIRKY AND QUIETLY CONFIDENT. A BIT LAST CENTURY, THOUGH.

FLAT WHITE
TECH-SAVVY DEDICATED FOLLOWER OF FASHION. QUITE PLEASANT THOUGH. INTENDS TO DO SOME TRAVELING SHORTLY.

DECAF
THAT'S QUITE ENOUGH READING FOR YOU – IT'S WELL PAST YOUR BEDTIME.

DESIGN YOUR FAVORITE DOUGHNUT

COLOR IN THE DOUGHNUT:

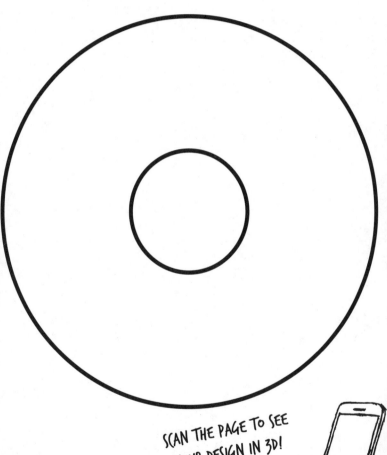

SCAN THE PAGE TO SEE YOUR DESIGN IN 3D!

DOODLE

FILL THIS PAGE WITH DOODLES

MAKE A COLLAGE USING YOUR FAVORITE
PARTS OF A MAGAZINE OR NEWSPAPER

MY GOALS

USE THIS PAGE AND THE NEXT TO FILL IN WHAT YOU'D LIKE TO ACHIEVE:

IN THE NEXT MINUTE:

_____

_____

_____

_____

IN THE NEXT HALF HOUR:

_____

_____

_____

_____

BY THE END OF THE DAY:

_____

_____

_____

_____

BY THE END OF THE WEEK:

_____

_____

_____

_____

BY THE END OF THE MONTH:

_____

_____

_____

_____

IN THE NEXT YEAR:

_____

_____

_____

_____

IN THE NEXT TEN YEARS:

_____

_____

_____

_____

BEFORE YOU DIE:

_____

_____

_____

_____

WORD SEARCH

```
L C K Z W L Z D C O G X
U I C A Y G X O O S P Y
I R W A O U O Q O J L E
O N E S M G F L Y M C N
D L N G U E N O H P C I
L M O P A D R E Q X Q L
E S R R I H K A S O Z O
U A D B Y B I R X T Z P
Z F O E D I V S M Q K M
P G W A M J W R M X J A
Q T R C Z W Y F U N M R
Q X N H C O L E V A R T
```

CAMERA	PUG
DRONE	FUN
PHONE	ZOOM
TRAVEL	TRAMPOLINE
VIDEO	BEACH

PIZZA IN A MUG RECIPE...

INGREDIENTS:

4 TBSP PLAIN FLOUR

1/8 TSP BAKING POWDER

PINCH OF SALT

PINCH OF BAKING SODA

3 TBSP MILK

1 TBSP SUNFLOWER OIL

NICE TOMATO-BASED PASTA SAUCE

GRATED CHEESE

FEW SLICES OF PEPPERONI (OR ANY TOPPING OF YOUR CHOICE).

METHOD:

GRAB YOURSELF A MUG. MAKE SURE IT CAN GO IN THE MICROWAVE.

MIX THE FLOUR, BAKING POWDER, SALT, BAKING SODA, MILK, CHEESE AND OIL TOGETHER WITH A FORK OR A SMALL WHISK.

ADD THE TOMATO PASTA SAUCE, CHEESE AND OTHER TOPPING.

STICK IN THE MICROWAVE ON HIGH FOR 60–80 SECONDS.

ENJOY!

SCAN THE PAGE TO WATCH ALFIE IN ACTION

TRY TO BE THE
RAINBOW IN
SOMEONE'S CLOUD.

(MAYA ANGELOU)

EVEN NEWER BRAINTEASERS

1. A MAN PUSHES HIS CAR TO A HOTEL AND TELLS ITS OWNER THAT HE IS BANKRUPT. WHY?

_____

2. YOU HAVE A 3-GALLON JUG AND A 5-GALLON JUG. YOU NEED TO MEASURE OUT EXACTLY 7 GALLONS OF WATER. HOW CAN YOU DO IT?

_____

3. WHAT WORDS ARE PRONOUNCED DIFFERENTLY BY SIMPLY CAPITALIZING THE FIRST LETTER? I'LL GIVE YOU A CLUE: TWO OF THE WORDS ARE CITIES AND ONE OF THE WORDS IS A EUROPEAN NATIONALITY.

_____

4. HOW FAR CAN A RABBIT RUN INTO THE WOODS?

_____

5. WHAT IS FULL OF HOLES BUT CAN STILL HOLD WATER?

_____

TELEPATHY EXERCISE 1

YOU'LL NEED A FRIEND WHO HAS ALSO VERY SENSIBLY BOUGHT THIS
BOOK. NOW, THINK OF A PERSON AND TELL YOUR FRIEND TO DO THE
SAME. TRY AND DRAW THE PERSON YOUR FRIEND IS THINKING OF!

TELEPATHY EXERCISE 2

FOR THIS ONE, YOU'LL NEED A FRIEND. NOW, THINK OF AN ANIMAL AND TELL YOUR FRIEND TO DO THE SAME. TRY AND DRAW THE ANIMAL YOUR FRIEND IS THINKING OF!

SCAN THE PAGE AND WATCH ALFIE'S ATTEMPT

MINDFULNESS EXERCISE

HERE'S A REALLY GOOD ONE TO RELIEVE
TENSION: CLENCH YOUR HANDS REALLY
TIGHTLY AND HOLD THEM FOR 10 SECONDS,
THEN RELAX. FOCUS ON HOW YOUR HANDS
FEEL AND CONCENTRATE ON THE FEELING
FOR AS LONG AS YOU CAN.

RANDOM PIZZA TOPPING

LIST 5 NICE TOPPINGS AND 5 NASTY TOPPINGS BELOW.
CUT THEM OUT AND PICK OUT 5 TO SEE WHAT YOU'VE
ENDED UP WITH. AND THEN JUST HOPE YOU DON'T
HAVE TO EAT IT...

NICE TOPPINGS   NASTY TOPPINGS

FILL IN THE GAPS TO CREATE EXPRESSIONS THAT ARE BETTER THAN THE ORIGINAL ONES

1. _____ IS WORTH 1,000 WORDS

2. THE BEST THING SINCE _____

3. DON'T JUDGE _____ BY ITS _____

4. IT TAKES TWO TO _____

5. LET THE CAT OUT OF THE _____

IT ALWAYS SEEMS IMPOSSIBLE UNTIL IT'S DONE

(NELSON MANDELA)

FILL IN THE GAPS TO CREATE YOUR OWN BOOK TITLES

THE LION, THE WITCH AND THE _____

ONE HUNDRED YEARS OF _____

ALICE'S ADVENTURES IN _____

THE SOUND AND THE _____

THE LORD OF THE _____

SCAN THE PAGE TO SEE
ALFIE'S TITLES

CURRENTLY I'M...

TRYING TO GET THIS OUT OF MY HEAD:

WAITING FOR:

WANTING TO WATCH THIS SHOW:

FEELING POSITIVE ABOUT:

LOOKING FORWARD TO:

CURRENTLY I'M DREAMING ABOUT GOING TO THESE 5 PLACES:

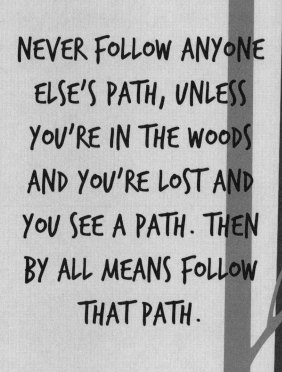

NEVER FOLLOW ANYONE ELSE'S PATH, UNLESS YOU'RE IN THE WOODS AND YOU'RE LOST AND YOU SEE A PATH. THEN BY ALL MEANS FOLLOW THAT PATH.

(ELLEN DE GENERES)

HERE ARE SOME SELFIE PROPS FOR YOU TO CUT OUT

IT ALL STARTED THE DAY I WENT TO AN OLD ANTIQUE SHOP IN TOWN AND DISCOVERED A...

MAKE UP A SHORT STORY AND WRITE IT AROUND THE EDGE OF THIS PAGE

CATCHPHRASE 1

IT'S TIME FOR A CLASSIC GAME OF GUESS THE BAND
FROM THE VISUAL CLUES BELOW...

1.

2.

_____

_____

3.

4.

_____

_____

CATCHPHRASE 2

GUESS THE TITLE OF THE TV SHOW FROM THE CLUES BELOW...

1.

2.
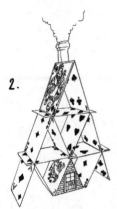

_____

_____

3.
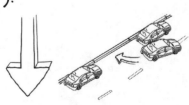

4.

_____

_____

GUESS THE YOUTUBER

WHO AM I?

1. MY BIGGEST FEAR IS BEES.

2. I'VE FAILED THE 120 CHICKEN NUGGET CHALLENGE WITH ALFIE TWICE.

3. MY FIRST JOB WAS IN A RETAIL STORE.

4. MY FAVORITE TOY GROWING UP WAS A RED ELEPHANT.

5. I'VE BROKEN MY ELBOW THREE TIMES

6. WHEN I HIT 100,000 FOLLOWERS, I STOOD ON TOP OF A PLANE AND DID WING WALKING!

7. I TOOK ONLINE DANCE LESSONS ON YOUTUBE

HOT CHOCOLATE MUG BROWNIE RECIPE (EGG-FREE)

INGREDIENTS

6 TBSP HOT CHOCOLATE POWDER

4 TBSP PLAIN FLOUR

2 TBSP MELTED BUTTER

3 TBSP WATER

1/2 TSP VANILLA EXTRACT

HANDFUL OF CHOCOLATE CHIPS

METHOD

GRAB YOURSELF A MUG AND MAKE SURE IT CAN GO IN THE MICROWAVE.

MIX THE POWDER AND FLOUR, BEFORE STIRRING IN THE OIL, WATER AND VANILLA ESSENCE WITH A FORK. ADD THE CHOCOLATE CHIPS.

STICK IN THE MICROWAVE ON HIGH FOR 60-90 SECONDS.

ALLOW TO COOL FOR A FEW MINUTES AND ENJOY!

FITNESS CHALLENGE

1. DO AS MANY PUSH UPS AS YOU CAN IN 1 MINUTE.

2. PLANK - SEE HOW LONG YOU CAN HOLD A PLANK FOR. IT'S NOT EASY AS IT LOOKS!

3. AND HERE'S A SILLY ONE: SEE HOW SLOWLY YOU CAN WALK DOWN YOUR STREET.

EXPECTATION VS REALITY

IN THE BOXES BELOW, CUT OUT AND PASTE PICTURES OF WHAT YOU WANTED ON
THE LEFT AND WHAT YOU ACTUALLY GOT ON THE RIGHT.

EXAM RESULTS: WHAT I WANTED	EXAM RESULTS: WHAT I ACTUALLY GOT
MY WEEKEND: WHAT I WANTED TO DO	MY WEEKEND: WHAT ACTUALLY HAPPENED

BEACH

CREATE A PARTY OUTFIT USING CANDY WRAPPERS

INSTEAD OF THROWING YOUR
CANDY WRAPPERS AWAY, CUT AND
STICK THEM TO THE MANNEQUIN
TO CREATE AN OUTFIT.

ART BY ERIN DOWNES

HOW WELL DOES MY BEST FRIEND KNOW ME?

ASK YOUR BEST FRIEND TO WRITE DOWN THE ANSWERS TO THE QUESTIONS BELOW AND HAND IT BACK TO YOU TO MARK.

1. WHAT IS THEIR FAVORITE CHOCOLATE BAR?

2. WHERE WERE THEY BORN?

3. WHAT IS THE FIRST CONCERT THEY ATTENDED?

4. IF THEY WENT TO A FANCY DRESS PARTY AND COULD DRESS UP AS ANYONE OR ANYTHING, WHAT WOULD THEY CHOOSE?

5. WHAT IS THEIR IDEAL TAKEOUT ORDER?

6. WHERE DO THEY WANT TO GO ON HOLIDAY?

7. IF THEY COULD GO ON A DATE WITH ANYONE, WHO WOULD IT BE?

8. WHICH ACTOR OR ACTRESS WOULD THEY WANT TO PLAY THEM IN A FILM ABOUT THEIR LIVES?

9. WHAT IS THEIR FAVORITE YOUTUBE VIDEO?

10. WHEN DID THE TWO OF YOU LAST HAVE AN ARGUMENT?

SCORES

10 POINTS FOR A CORRECT ANSWER
5 POINTS FOR A PRETTY CLOSE ANSWER

50 OR ABOVE – IT'S OFFICIAL. BFFS FOREVER.

25–50 – LET'S GET TO KNOW EACH OTHER BETTER.

0–25 – YOU HAVE PERMISSION TO PUSH A PAPER/
CARDBOARD PLATE OF WHIPPED CREAM INTO YOUR
'FRIEND'S' FACE.

BEST FRIEND QUICK FIRE QUESTIONS

1. CAT OR DOG?

2. PIZZA OR BURGER?

3. BOOK OR FILM?

4. BEACH OR POOL?

5. SINGING OR DANCING?

6. STRAWBERRY OR CHOCOLATE?

7. YOUTUBE OR FACEBOOK?

8. INSIDE OR OUTSIDE?

9. POP OR ROCK?

10.

11.

12.

DRAW YOUR OWN POINTLESS EMOJI

GO AND COLLECT 10 THINGS FROM
THE OUTSIDE WORLD ASSOCIATED
WITH THE LETTER...

THE TRY NOT TO LAUGH CHALLENGE REVISITED

WRITE DOWN 4 YOUTUBE VIDEOS THAT REALLY MAKE YOU LAUGH.
THEN CHALLENGE YOUR FRIEND TO WATCH THEM AND SEE HOW
LONG IT TAKES UNTIL THEY CRACK UP!

1.

2.

3.

4.

NEW YOGA POSITIONS TO LEARN

(ONLY ATTEMPT THESE WITH PROPER TRAINING TO AVOID INJURY!)

 THE CROW

THE WHEEL

 KING DANCER

 THE LOTUS

THE TREE

 THE FLYING
PLANK

IN TEN YEARS...

LET'S SEE WHAT YOU THINK YOU WILL BE DOING TEN YEARS FROM NOW...

WHERE WILL YOU BE LIVING IN TEN YEARS?

WHO WILL YOU BE LIVING WITH IN TEN YEARS?

WHAT WILL BE YOUR FAVORITE FOOD IN TEN YEARS?

HOW OLD WILL YOU BE IN TEN YEARS?

WHO WILL BE YOUR FAVORITE YOUTUBER IN TEN YEARS?

WHERE WILL YOU HAVE TRAVELED IN TEN YEARS?

WHAT WILL BE YOUR FAVORITE DRINK IN TEN YEARS?

WHAT WILL BE YOUR JOB IN TEN YEARS?

WHAT MUSIC WILL YOU BE LISTENING TO IN TEN YEARS?

WATER CHALLENGE

PROBABLY BEST TO PLAY THIS ONE OUTSIDE. YOU WILL NEED:

A DECK OF CARDS

A SHOT GLASS

A TEACUP

A VASE

A BUCKET FILLED WITH COLD WATER

SIT OPPOSITE A FRIEND AND SHUFFLE THE DECK OF CARDS.

YOU WILL TAKE TURNS DRAWING A CARD FROM THE TOP OF THE DECK. HIGH CARD WINS.

IF YOU LOSE ONCE, YOUR FRIEND GETS TO THROW THE WATER IN A SHOT GLASS AT YOU.

IF YOU LOSE TWICE, IT'S A TEACUP, AND SO ON.

THE LOSER IS THE ONE WHO GETS THE BUCKET OF WATER THROWN ON THEM.

MINDFULNESS EXERCISE

FOR THIS EXERCISE, IN A QUIET ROOM,
SELECT A RANDOM SONG THAT YOU HAVE NEVER
HEARD BEFORE. TRY NOT TO JUDGE THE PIECE OF MUSIC BASED
ON THE ARTIST, TITLE OR STYLE OF MUSIC.

ALLOW YOURSELF TO EXPLORE EVERY ASPECT OF THE SONG. PAY
ATTENTION TO THE DIFFERENT INSTRUMENTS, THE TONE OF THE
SINGER'S VOICE AND THE THOUGHT THAT HAS GONE INTO MAKING
IT. THE POINT OF THIS IS TO JUST LISTEN AND BECOME FULLY
IMMERSED IN THE COMPOSITION WITHOUT BEING
CLOUDED BY YOUR PAST EXPERIENCES.

WRITE DOWN YOUR WORST FEARS

(IF YOU WRITE THEM DOWN THEY MAY NOT SEEM SO SCARY...)

1.

2.

3.

4.

5.

RIDDLES

CAN YOU SOLVE THESE RIDDLES?

1. WHAT WALKS ON 4 LEGS WHEN IT IS MORNING, ON 2 LEGS AT NOON AND ON 3 LEGS IN THE EVENING?

_____

2. THIS IS A THING THAT IS DEVOURED BY ALL THINGS — FLOWERS, TREES, BEASTS, BIRDS; BITES STEEL, GNAWS IRON; GRINDS HARD STONE TO METAL; BEATS MOUNTAINS DOWN, RUINS TOWNS AND SLAYS KINGS. WHAT IS IT?

_____

3. THERE IS A HOUSE. A PERSON ENTERS THIS HOUSE BLIND BUT EXITS ABLE TO SEE. WHAT IS IT?

_____

GO AND COLLECT 10 THINGS FROM
THE OUTSIDE WORLD ASSOCIATED
WITH THE LETTER...

WRITE DOWN YOUR FAVORITE EVER:

1. FOOD

2. FILM

3. BOOK

4. SONG

5. PLACE

6. MEMORY WITH FRIENDS

7. MOMENT IN YOUR LIFE

SCAN THE PAGE FOR ALFIE'S FAVORITES

YOUR CALM MIND
IS THE ULTIMATE
WEAPON AGAINST
YOUR CHALLENGES.
SO RELAX.

(BRYANT MCGILL)

WOULD YOU RATHER...

1. GIVE UP CHEESE OR CHOCOLATE?

2. BE ITCHY FOR THE REST OF YOUR LIFE OR BE STICKY FOR THE REST OF YOUR LIFE?

3. LOSE ALL YOUR MONEY AND VALUABLES OR ALL THE PICTURES YOU'VE EVER TAKEN?

4. GIVE UP SOCIAL MEDIA OR TV?

5. BE FEARED BY EVERYONE OR LOVED BY EVERYONE?

6. BE ABLE TO CONTROL FIRE OR WATER?

7. BE A FAMOUS ACTOR/ACTRESS OR A FAMOUS DIRECTOR?

8. EITHER NEVER GET A PAPER CUT AGAIN OR NEVER GET A SPLINTER AGAIN?

9. FLY LIKE SUPERMAN OR SWING LIKE SPIDER-MAN?

POINTLESS EYE SPY

WHEN YOU SEE SOMETHING BEGINNING WITH ANY OF THE LETTERS BELOW, WRITE IT DOWN!

A=

B=

C=

D=

E=

F=

G=

H=

I=

J=

K=

L=

M=

N=

O=

P=

Q=

R=

S=

T=

U=

V=

W=

X=

Y=

Z=

LOVE WHERE YOU LIVE

WRITE DOWN YOUR FAVORITE THINGS ABOUT WHERE YOU LIVE:

AND ONE PLACE YOU'D LIKE TO VISIT:

AND ONE OF YOUR FAVORITE MEMORIES:

INTERVIEW WITH A FRIEND

THIS IS ALL ABOUT FINDING OUT ABOUT EACH OTHER AND EXPLORING YOUR RELATIONSHIP. SIMPLY GRAB A FRIEND AND ASK THEM QUESTIONS ABOUT THEIR LIFE. WHERE WERE THEY BORN? WHAT WAS THEIR FIRST JOB? WHERE DO THEY WANT TO BE IN 5 YEARS, 10 YEARS, 50 YEARS?

WEIRD FOOD COMBINATIONS

WRITE DOWN WHAT WEIRD THINGS YOU LIKE TO EAT:

E.G. OLIVES AND NOODLES

E.G. CHIPS DIPPED IN CHOCOLATE

SCAN THE PAGE FOR ALFIE'S COMBINATIONS

FOOD TRUTH OR DARE

TAKE TURNS ASKING 'TRUTH OR DARE'? TO A FRIEND.
YOU CAN FILL OUT THE 'TRUTH' QUESTIONS TO ASK. AS FOR THE
DARES, LOOK BACK TO THE WEIRD FOOD COMBINATION PAGE!

TRUTH

1.

2.

3.

4.

5.

XMAS LIST

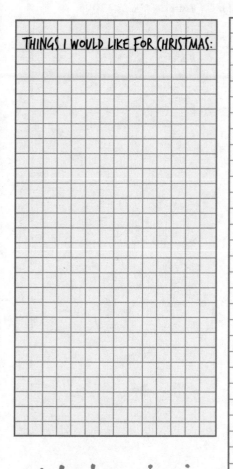

THINGS I WOULD LIKE FOR CHRISTMAS:

THINGS I NEED TO REMEMBER TO
BUY OTHER PEOPLE:

MAKE UP A STORY USING THESE WORDS

YOU DON'T HAVE TO USE ONLY THESE WORDS, BUT THESE WORDS ABSOLUTELY NEED TO FEATURE.

KEBAB

SERENITY

BLINK

CANOE

SQUIRTY

PUG

CHALLENGE

DAFFODIL

GLOBULE

WEDDING

CRAFT

TWILIGHT

HEADPHONES

POINTLESS

MUFFIN

MAKE UP A STORY BUT YOU'RE NOT ALLOWED TO USE THESE WORDS

THESE ARE THE 10 MOST COMMONLY USED WORDS ACCORDING TO THE OXFORD ENGLISH DICTIONARY. MAKE UP A STORY WITHOUT USING ANY OF THEM!

THE

BE

TO

OF

AND

A

IN

THAT

HAVE

I

SCAN THE PAGE TO WATCH ALFIE'S STORY

SIGN LANGUAGE PHRASES

BEAR

BULL

MONKEY

LION

HERE ARE SOME COUNTRY NAMES WITH A FEW LETTERS MISSING. CAN YOU GUESS THE NAMES?

H _ _ T I

_ O R _ C C _

L _ E C H _ E N _ T _ I N

K _ _ _ I T

_ _ R A I _ E

Z I _ _ A _ _ E

_ _ J I

_ E R _ _ N Y

C _ L O _ B _ A

DISGUSTING DICE CHALLENGE

CUT OUT THE PAPER CUBE TEMPLATE ON THE FACING PAGE. FOLD ALONG THE LINES AND TAPE IT TOGETHER TO MAKE THE DICE.

WRITE DOWN SIX DISGUSTING THINGS THAT YOU OR WHOEVER ROLLS THE DICE HAS TO DO IF THAT NUMBER COMES UP.

DICE WITH NUMBER 1

_____

DICE WITH NUMBER 2

_____

DICE WITH NUMBER 3

_____

DICE WITH NUMBER 4

_____

DICE WITH NUMBER 5

_____

DICE WITH NUMBER 6

_____

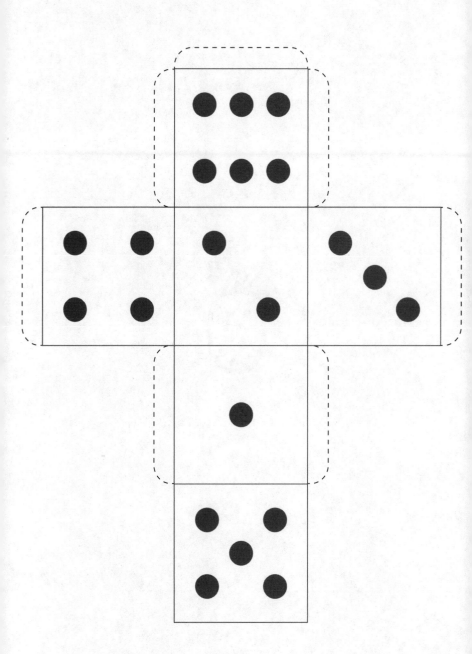

WE DO NOT NEED MAGIC
TO TRANSFORM OUR WORLD.
WE CARRY ALL OF THE
POWER WE NEED INSIDE
OURSELVES ALREADY.

(J.K. ROWLING)

TAKE A PHOTO OF WHAT YOU
THINK DEFINES HAPPINESS
AND STICK IT HERE

THE POINTLESS PUN GAME

GUESS THE PUN ON THE FILM TITLE FROM THE CLUES BELOW:

1. PIECE OF STEAK AND A MOTHER AND FATHER HOLDING HANDS.

(MEAT THE PARENTS)

2. A CARTON OF YOGURT IN A SCHOOL LOCKER. (CLUE: IT'S A WAR FILM.)

3. TWO HOT DOG BUNS, WITH AN ARROW POINTING TO THE TOP ONE.
   (CLUE: THINK TOM CRUISE)

4. A SHRIMP LOOKING IN A MIRROR WITH A QUESTION MARK OVER ITS HEAD.
   THE SHRIMP IS CARRYING A PASSPORT. (CLUE: THINK MATT DAMON)

5. A MAN WEARING A CROWN AND A PEACH. (CLUE: THINK COLIN FIRTH))

DRAW YOUR OWN SELFIE

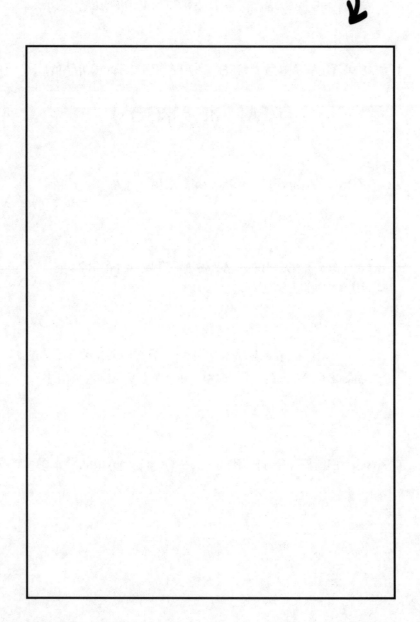

THE DREAM JAR

WRITE DOWN YOUR DREAMS ON THE STRIPS BELOW, CUT THEM UP AND PLACE THEM IN A JAR. CHECK THEM EXACTLY ONE YEAR TO THE DAY.

IF ANY OF THEM HAVE COME TRUE, PUT THEM IN A SPECIAL PLACE OR IMMORTALIZE THEM IN A PICTURE FRAME. YOU CAN DECORATE THE JAR AND THE STRIPS OF PAPER HOWEVER YOU LIKE.

DREAM 1.

DREAM 2.

DREAM 3.

DREAM 4.

DREAM 5.

DREAM 6.

DREAM 7.

DREAM 8.

DREAM 9.

DREAM 10.

BOGGLE

IF YOU HAVEN'T PLAYED BOGGLE BEFORE, THE IDEA IS TO FIND WORDS
ON THE GRID BELOW WHICH ARE FORMED FROM LETTERS THAT ARE
IMMEDIATELY NEXT TO EACH OTHER (HORIZONTALLY, VERTICALLY OR
DIAGONALLY). YOU MAY BE ABLE TO SPOT ONE WORD STRAIGHTAWAY!

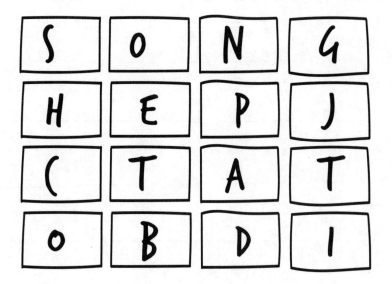

31-DAY WRITING CHALLENGE

EACH DAY FOR THE NEXT MONTH, WRITE DOWN ONE THING
THAT MADE YOU HAPPY THAT DAY.

DAY 1

_____

DAY 2

_____

DAY 3

_____

DAY 4

_____

DAY 5

_____

DAY 6

_____

DAY 7

_____

DAY 8

_____

DAY 9

_____

DAY 10

DAY 11

DAY 12

DAY 13

DAY 14

DAY 15

DAY 16

DAY 17

DAY 18

DAY 19

DAY 20

DAY 21

_____

DAY 22

_____

DAY 23

_____

DAY 24

_____

DAY 25

_____

DAY 26

_____

DAY 27

_____

DAY 28

_____

DAY 29

_____

DAY 30

_____

DAY 31

_____

WHAT I CAN CONTROL
WITH MY LIFE

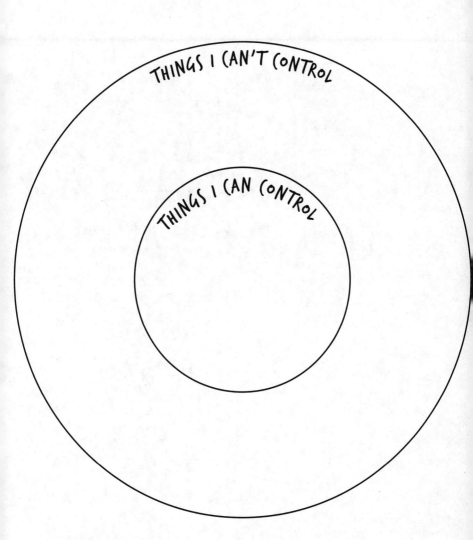

THINGS I CAN'T CONTROL

THINGS I CAN CONTROL

DON'T CALL IT A DREAM, CALL IT A PLAN

DESK BASKETBALL

MAKE A HOLE BY CUTTING OUT THE CIRCLE BELOW. LAY THE PIECE OF PAPER DOWN OVER A MUG AND PRACTICE SHOOTING SOME HOOPS.

CRUMPLE UP THE BOTTOM THIRD OF THE PAGE TO MAKE YOUR BALL.

BEGINNING AND END OF YEAR JOURNAL

I SPENT THE FIRST DAY OF THE YEAR...

THESE ARE THE NEW YEAR'S RESOLUTIONS I MADE:

☐

☐

☐

☐

☐

I SPENT THE LAST DAY OF THE YEAR...

PEOPLE WATCHING GAME

CHECK WHEN YOU SEE:

A PERSON WEARING RED TROUSERS ☐

A PERSON WEARING A SOCCER SCARF ☐

SOMEONE CARRYING TOO MANY SHOPPING BAGS ☐

A PERSON LOOKING EXCEPTIONALLY PLEASED
WITH THEIR PURCHASE ☐

A PIGEON CHASING ANOTHER PIGEON ☐

SOMEONE CARRYING AN ITEM OF FOOD
THAT YOU'D LIKE ☐

SOMEONE CLEARLY LOOKING LOST ☐

DRAW YOUR OWN GAME CHARACTER!

SCAN THE PAGE TO SEE
ALFIE'S CHARACTER

IF YOUR LIFE WAS A SONG, WRITE THE CHORUS:

THE TEACUP CHALLENGE

THIS IS POSSIBLY THE MOST INFURIATING
YET ADDICTIVE GAME YET.

ITEMS NEEDED:

SEVERAL TEABAGS

MARKSMANSHIP

COMPETITIVE SPIRIT

INHUMAN SUPPLY OF PATIENCE

INSTRUCTIONS:

PLACE A MUG UNDER A HEAD-HEIGHT KITCHEN CUPBOARD. ATTEMPT
TO BOUNCE THE TEABAG OFF THE CUPBOARD AND INTO THE MUG
FROM A DISTANCE OF YOUR CHOOSING.

SCAN THE PAGE TO SEE
ALFIE'S ATTEMPT

SET YOURSELF 5 BOOKS YOU REALLY WANT TO READ IN THE NEXT MONTH...

1.

2.

3.

4.

5.

READ THEM WITH YOUR FRIENDS AND COMPARE NOTES.

WORRY REMOVAL SERVICE

WRITE DOWN ANY CURRENT AND FUTURE WORRIES ON THESE HANDY STRIPS BELOW. THEN CUT THEM OUT AND CHUCK THEM AWAY. PROBLEMS SOLVED!

FUNNY PARAGRAPH CHALLENGE

WORK OUT THE ANSWERS TO THESE QUESTIONS AND RIDDLES, AND USE THEM ON THE FOLLOWING PAGE TO HELP CREATE A FUNNY PARAGRAPH.

COMPLETE THIS EXPRESSION: TO _____ AND TO HOLD.

COMPLETE THIS EXPRESSION: A WATCHED POT _____ BOILS.

WHAT'S ANOTHER WORD FOR "GIGGLED" OR "CHUCKLED"?

WHAT IS THE OPPOSITE OF SOFT?

WHAT DOES A DOG DO WHEN IT'S HOT?

WHAT IS THE TRANSLATION OF THE FRENCH WORD 'TOILETTE'?

COMPLETE THIS EXPRESSION: TO GET ONE'S _____ OUT OF JOINT.

TURN OVER TO FILL THEM IN ⟶

INSERT FUNNY PARAGRAPH HERE

CHARADES

CUT OUT EACH ONE OF THE WORDS BELOW, FOLD IT OVER AND PUT THEM IN A LARGE MUG. PICK OUT ONE AND THEN ACT IT OUT TO YOUR FRIENDS WITHOUT USING WORDS OR LIP MOVEMENTS. YOU HAVE 60 SECONDS TO ACT OUT EACH WORD.

MILKSHAKE	STATUE OF LIBERTY
HOT DOG	YO-YO
HARRY STYLES	BUBBLE GUM
THE QUEEN	SUNGLASSES
BAMBI	ICE SKATING

DESIGN YOUR OWN FACE FILTER

COLOR IN THE CAP AND WATCH IT TRANSFORM INTO YOUR PERSONAL FACE FILTER.

SCAN THE PAGE AND TAKE A SELFIE

CHINESE WHISPERS PICTIONARY

THIS IS A GREAT VARIATION ON PICTIONARY.
IDEALLY, YOU NEED (AT LEAST) FIVE PLAYERS.

IT STARTS LIKE PICTIONARY WITH SOMEONE DRAWING A PICTURE
OF ONE OF THE WORDS WRITTEN BELOW. THEN A SECOND PERSON
NEEDS TO GUESS WHAT YOU HAVE DRAWN (WITHOUT ANYONE
ELSE CONTRIBUTING) AND WRITE THEIR GUESS ON A SEPARATE
PIECE OF PAPER.

THIS GUESS IS THEN PASSED TO A THIRD PERSON WHO DRAWS A
PICTURE OF IT ON ANOTHER PIECE OF PAPER. A FOURTH PERSON
GUESSES WHAT THE THIRD PERSON HAS DRAWN AND WRITES THEIR
GUESS DOWN ON ANOTHER PIECE OF PAPER. THIS PIECE OF PAPER
IS PASSED TO THE FIFTH PERSON TO DRAW A PICTURE OF IT. THIS IS
SHOWN TO THE FIRST PERSON WHO GUESSES WHAT HAS BEEN DRAWN.
GATHER ALL THE PIECES OF PAPER AND SEE HOW FAR AWAY FROM
THE ORIGINAL INTENDED DRAWING YOU ARE!

THE LORD OF THE RINGS

THE DARK KNIGHT RISES

THE MUPPET CHRISTMAS CAROL

ONE FLEW OVER THE CUCKOO'S NEST

LOST IN TRANSLATION

ORANGE IS THE NEW BLACK

SUDOKU

			8			9	3	
	1	8		4				7
9	4				6	2		
1		6		3			9	
	5		6					3
		2	9		7		6	8
		4	7					
3								6
			1	2		5		

ANSWER PAGES

PAGE 21

DINGBATS

1. UP FOR GRABS
2. HEAD IN THE SAND
3. AMBIGUOUS
4. SCRAMBLED EGGS
5. ON THE RIGHT SIDE OF THE LAW

PAGE 22

JUMBLED PARAGRAPH

IF YOU COME DOWN TO BRIGHTON,
BE SURE TO GET YOURSELF AN ICE CREAM.
A WORD OF WARNING, THOUGH. ALWAYS
KEEP ONE EYE ON YOUR 99 OR A SEAGULL
WILL NICK IT. THE SAME APPLIES TO FISH
AND CHIPS, CANDY FLOSS AND ROCK!

PAGE 24

POINTLESS ANAGRAMS

GOOD MORNING GUYS!
SCRAPBOOK OF MY LIFE
DO MORE OF WHAT MAKES YOU HAPPY
POINTLESS BOOK THREE

PAGE 40

A TRICKY QUIZ

1. 12
2. BECAUSE HE'S DEAD!
3. ADAM
4. MOUNT EVEREST
5. THEY SLEEP AT NIGHT!

PAGE 46-47

PICTURE PUNS

1. GRATEFUL
2. KETTLE OF FISH
3. TOUCAN PLAY THAT GAME
4. ENCOURAGE MINT
5. BREAKFAST IN BED
6. ZOMBEE
7. PORK CHOP
8. PUNKTUATION

PAGE 51

10 NEW WORDS

1. A   6. I
2. E   7. B
3. F   8. C
4. D   9. J
5. H   10. G

PAGE 58

MAZE CHALLENGE

PAGE 80

NEW BRAINTEASERS

1. THE DICTIONARY
2. A COAT OF PAINT
3. A PILLOW
4. SILENCE
5. CHARCOAL

PAGE 81

CROSSWORD

ACROSS	DOWN
1. SPANISH	1. SICILY
2. CALIFORNIA	3. FINLAND
7. ITALY	4. JAPAN
5. LISBON	6. EQUATOR
9. BRAZIL	8. SEINE

PAGE 96

WORDSEARCH

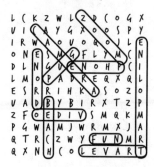

PAGE 99

EVEN NEWER BRAINTEASERS

1. HE'S PLAYING MONOPOLY

2. FILL THE 5-GALLON JUG AND POUR IT INTO THE 3-GALLON JUG. YOU NOW HAVE 2 GALLONS LEFT IN THE 5-GALLON JUG. NOW FILL THE 5-GALLON JUG UP TO THE TOP. YOU NOW HAVE 7 GALLONS.

3. READING, READING; NICE, NICE; POLISH, POLISH

4. HALFWAY; AFTER THAT THE RABBIT IS RUNNING OUT OF THE WOODS

5. A SPONGE

PAGE 116-117

CATCHPHRASES

BANDS

1. RED HOT CHILLI PEPPERS
2. ARTIC MONKEYS
3. BLACK EYED PEAS
4. VAMPIRE WEEKEND

TV SHOWS

1. HOMELAND
2. HOUSE OF CARDS
3. SOUTH PARK
4. BROADCHURCH

PAGE 118

GUESS THE YOUTUBER

MARCUS BUTLER

PAGE 137

RIDDLES

1. A HUMAN – A CHILD CRAWLS ON 4 LEGS, WALKS ON 2 AS AN ADULT AND WALKS WITH A CANE AS AN OLD PERSON, HENCE 3 LEGS.

2. TIME

3. A SCHOOL

PAGE 153

GUESS THE COUNTRIES

HAITI
MOROCCO
LIECHTENSTEIN
KUWAIT
UKRAINE
ZIMBABWE
FIJI
GERMANY
COLOMBIA

PAGE 159

THE POINTLESS PUN GAME

1. MEAT THE PARENTS
2. THE YOGHURT LOCKER
3. TOP BUN
4. THE PRAWN IDENTITY
5. THE KING'S PEACH

PAGE 181

FUNNY PARAGRAPH CHALLENGE

HAVE
NEVER
LAUGHED
HARD
PANTS
TOILET
NOSE

PAGE 189

SUDOKU

6	7	5	8	1	2	9	3	4
2	1	8	3	4	9	6	5	7
9	4	3	5	7	6	2	8	1
1	8	6	2	3	4	7	9	5
7	5	9	6	8	1	4	2	3
4	3	2	9	5	7	1	6	8
5	9	4	7	6	8	3	1	2
3	2	1	4	9	5	8	7	6
8	6	7	1	2	3	5	4	9